A Mother's Love

Amy Newmark

CSS

Chicken Soup for the Soul, LLC
Cos Cob, CT

Chicken Soup for the Soul: A Mother's Love
Amy Newmark

Published by Chicken Soup for the Soul, LLC www.chickensoup.com

Copyright ©2017 by Chicken Soup for the Soul, LLC. All Rights Reserved.

The publisher gratefully acknowledges the many publishers and individuals who granted Chicken Soup for the Soul permission to reprint the cited material.

Front cover photo courtesy of iStockPhoto.com/digitalskillet (©digitalskillet).
Back cover and interior photo courtesy of photos.com.

Interior photo of Amy Newmark courtesy of Susan Morrow at SwickPix

Cover and Interior by Daniel Zaccari

ISBN: 978-1-61159-063-0

PRINTED IN THE UNITED STATES OF AMERICA
on acid∞free paper

25 24 23 22 21   03 04 05 06 07 08 09 10 11

Table of Contents

Mom to the Rescue

A mother's heart is a patchwork of love.
~Author Unknown

think my friends and I started planning our senior prom when we were freshmen. Seriously. We talked for hours about what we'd wear, how we'd do our hair, how we'd pose for our pictures — as couples, then in a group, just the girls, then just the guys — where we'd eat, even rehearsed what we might talk about at the restaurant. I know. Get a life. But it was that huge to us. We painstakingly choreographed every minute and, with all that planning, we expected nothing short of an idyllic prom experience.

The big day arrived and we started getting ready

before lunch. Between phone calls to each other, we worked on our hair, nails, make-up, shoes, dresses and purses. The restaurant where we'd made our reservations — three months ahead of time — was forty miles away. Ten of us were to meet there, three hours before the prom, eat together, then convoy to the dance.

The time came for my boyfriend, Rusty, to pick me up. No Rusty. Ten minutes passed. Still no sign of him. Twenty minutes. This was before cell phones so all I could do was wait — wait and experience a major meltdown. Thirty minutes. Forty. How could he do this to me? This was my only senior prom. He'd better be dead, I thought, or seriously injured. As my friends gathered in the restaurant, I paced the family room, burning a hole through the clock with my eyes. How could this happen? I'd planned everything so perfectly.

When Rusty finally peeled into our drive — an hour late — his tuxedo was rumpled and mottled with grease. The ruffled shirt was plastered to his chest with sweat. His face was flushed and his hair was tousled. He'd had a blowout on the interstate and had his first-ever tire changing experience only inches from rushing traffic. I tried to muster some sympathy for him but all I could see was my perfect prom night going down the toilet.

Little did I know that, while I was pacing the front room, my mom had been hard at work. She'd defrosted two steaks and roused my father to light the backyard grill. She'd gathered my grandmother's best china, crystal and lace tablecloth, thrown together an elegant dinner and then sent my little sister and nephew upstairs to don their Sunday best and serve as waiter and waitress.

By the time Rusty arrived, she'd transformed our living room into a private dining hall complete with candlelight and music. As our friends were returning from their formal dining experience, we were just sitting down to ours. I never saw Mama that night. She sent my sister and nephew through the door with dish after dish, from salad all the way to dessert. And while we ate, she washed, dried and ironed Rusty's tuxedo shirt.

We made it to prom with time to spare and a story to tell. Looking back now, I can't remember if I ever thanked my mom. I was probably more concerned with not spilling anything on my dress and making sure we got to the dance on time. She was content to remain in the shadows remedying yet another mini trauma in my life. By the way, thanks Mom.

~Mimi Greenwood Knight

The Sound of Music

Mothers and daughters are closest,
when daughters become mothers.
~Author Unknown

The words every mother dreads rang in my ears. "Mom, it might be cancer." How could this be? It's funny how life changes in an instant. One minute I was enjoying a newfound relationship with my grown daughter, and the next I was gripped with fear that it might all come to a tragic end.

Now that my daughter was grown, with children of her own, we had a bond that never existed before. Even though she and her husband moved all over the world, we stayed in touch by phone.

For the most part, the phone had been our lifeline to each other. Just being able to hear each other's voices bridged the time and distance between us.

I took that privilege for granted until a few years ago. After her first pregnancy my daughter developed an enlarged thyroid, and it was feared by the physicians that it might be cancerous. Surgery was scheduled, and her dad and I traveled clear across the United States to be with her. We didn't know what the surgeon would find inside our child's neck. When we met with him following the operation, he explained that the diseased thyroid had been wrapped around her vocal chords. He warned us that, although he was confident he had been careful, there was always the chance that her voice would be permanently damaged.

After strict orders not to talk, she embarked upon the process of healing. We flew home and waited for her voice to return. Little did I know how difficult the next few months would be. I had come to depend on our frequent phone conversations.

Now, I wondered if I would ever hear my daughter's voice again. We e-mailed back and forth, but it just wasn't the same. The biopsy results were negative for cancer, and we rejoiced. But still, we waited for the healing to be complete. I longed to hear her speak again.

At last I received a call from her — or was it her? Hearing the voice on the phone that day broke my heart. She could barely squeak out audible words, and I had a hard time believing it was my daughter. I could hear the thickness in her throat, and the high-pitched sounds were foreign. I cried as soon as we hung up. Was this how she would sound from now on? Did it hurt her to talk? I was afraid for her, and even scolded her about straining her voice by calling. But I didn't stop to think that she might have missed my voice as much as I did hers.

Over the next several months her voice gradually improved, until finally it was back to normal. I will always be grateful that it was not cancer, and that once again, we can share our lives though our phone conversations. We talk more often than ever now. Sometimes she rambles on and on. But I don't mind. The sound of her voice is music to my ears.

~Jan Cline

A Labor of Love

Happiness is not a goal; it is a by-product.
~Eleanor Roosevelt

M y mother carefully guided a piece of red fabric under the sewing machine needle. When she came to the end of the seam, she glanced at the clock and exclaimed, "It's four o'clock already? I have to start supper!" She jumped up from her chair and rushed to the kitchen.

The red cloth Mom set aside was going to be a dress for me. I needed something special to wear to my cousin's wedding, so every afternoon Mom sat at her Singer, the cabinet wedged halfway between the dining room and living room, right in the middle of all the commotion that came with having seven children. As soon as the needle started clicking, Mom went into a trance-like state, her face becoming more and more relaxed.

She hung the unfinished dress on a hanger in the dining room, and in the evening when my father came home he stopped to admire the work-in-progress as if it were a painting on an easel. First it was just a shell. The following day, dotted-Swiss sleeves appeared. A ruffled collar showed up next. "That's coming along nicely," Dad said, and Mom beamed.

By the end of the week, the dress was ready to be hemmed. As I slipped it over my head, goose bumps broke out on my arms, for this was the most beautiful dress my mother had ever made. I stood still on a chair while she held a yardstick to the lower edge and pulled straight pins from between her lips. She pinned up a few inches at a time, gradually moving around me until the pins in her mouth were gone and the hem was above my knee.

Mom hemmed the dress by hand, ironed out every wrinkle, and hung her masterpiece in the dining room one last time. "It's done," she announced with a sparkle in her eye, something that was missing when she mended torn crotches, darned my father's socks or stitched merit badges on my brothers' Boy Scout uniforms.

I couldn't remember a time my mother didn't sew. In the toy box were little dresses and bonnets she'd made for our baby dolls years ago. Clothing she'd crafted hung in every closet. She was always working on something: a bathrobe for Dad, a shirt for my brother, an angel costume for the youngest to wear on Halloween.

When the Home Economics teacher gave my tenth grade class an assignment to make a dress, I thought of my mother's handiwork and assumed it would be easy. I flipped through pattern books in the store and picked out a complicated design with a collar, cuffs and a twenty-two-inch zipper.

"Isn't this a cool dress?" I asked my mother.

"Maybe you ought to start with something simpler," she said.

I insisted and bought the pattern, along with a knit fabric, although my teacher had recommended cotton. When I got to school, I unfolded the directions and stared at the long list of steps. I didn't need directions. I'd seen my mother go through the process a thousand times.

I cut out the onionskin pattern pieces, pinned them to the fabric and snipped around them. After sewing my first seam, I gasped, "Oh, no! I sewed the wrong sides together!" The teacher handed me a seam ripper, and I grumbled as I tore out the stitches.

For weeks I struggled with the sleeves, collar and zipper. The knit fabric kept bunching up, and I daydreamed about sneaking my monstrosity home to Mom. She would have whipped it together in a few hours.

Finally I finished the dress, but unlike my mother's projects, you could tell mine was homemade. The collar didn't lie flat, and the zipper was bumpy. My teacher gave me a D plus, and she was probably being kind.

"Sewing is too much work!" I complained when I showed my mother the dress.

"My sewing is a labor of love," she said.

I rolled my eyes. I was sure she sewed because it would have cost a fortune to buy clothes in the store for seven kids.

My mother's sewing continued to be part of every stage of my life. She made a dress for my graduation from college, the bridesmaids' dresses for my wedding, and a maternity smock when I was pregnant with my first child. Inside every garment, Mom sewed a tag that said "Handmade by Betty." I still couldn't figure out why anyone would sew unless they had to.

One day, my husband told me that his mother had bought a new sewing machine and offered us her old one. He wanted to accept it so I could sew insignia on his Navy uniforms. Reluctantly, I agreed.

The pine cabinet sat unused in the corner of our bedroom for a long time.

Right after our second child was born, my husband went to sea and I was overwhelmed with taking care of the kids and house alone. My mother came for a visit, and although she didn't say anything about the idle sewing machine, after she left a package arrived in the mail from her. Inside were a new sewing basket and a pincushion that looked like a tomato.

Where would I find the energy to sew? I didn't need any more work!

A few days later, the kids were driving me crazy, and I wondered how my mother kept her sanity with seven children. I gazed at the sewing basket and remembered the peaceful look she always had on her face when she sewed. It was close to meditation, as if she were blocking out the world and gathering strength. "Let's go to the fabric store," I said to my son. I grabbed my purse and strapped the baby in her car seat.

At the store, I chose two patterns: one a simple sundress for my daughter, the other easy pajamas in my son's size. I found cotton printed with yellow roses for the sundress, and my son picked out some flannel with airplanes for his pajamas.

During the baby's nap, I ironed the cotton fabric, pinned the sundress pattern on it and cut out the pieces. Later, when my daughter was happy in her playpen, I dusted off the sewing cabinet, set up the machine and began to sew. The motor hummed and time flew. I felt focused and free.

The next day I finished the sundress and eagerly started on my son's pajamas. Creating clothing was so different from housework! It wasn't like a washed floor that my kids spilled juice on before I even put the bucket away. It wasn't like a big dinner that was quickly eaten, leaving a stack of dirty plates. I felt a sense of accomplishment when I made clothes for my kids. The final products were nowhere near the quality of my mother's work, yet somehow it didn't matter.

Years before, when my mother called her sewing "a labor of love," I thought she was saying it was a tedious job, but she did it anyway, out of love. But now I saw her sewing in another light. Not only did she do it with love, but she loved doing it!

~Mary Elizabeth Laufer

Love, Mom

A hundred hearts would be too few
To carry all my love for you.
~Author Unknown

can't say I was sad to see my daughter Zoey go to kindergarten. I love school so much that I have been continuously in school for three decades as either a student or a teacher. I'd say I was more excited for her than anything else. Zoey is like me — a rule follower, a bookworm, and a social butterfly. She entered kindergarten knowing how to read, and I was confident she'd enjoy every minute of school.

As I packed her lunch on the first morning, I decided I'd write a little note. I went to our dining room table, and I dug through the craft supplies. I found a piece of construction paper and some stickers. I created a very silly little card. I wrote, "Happy 1st Day of School Lovey Dovey! Have fun. Be good. Remember manners matter! Love, Mom." I did feel a small twinge as I thought of my little girl in a loud and chaotic cafeteria. I felt better knowing she'd open her lunchbox and see my note.

In the midst of telling us the details of her first day, we didn't think to ask about lunch or the note. However, as the days turned to weeks, I continued to make little cards — frequently related to the seasons or a holiday. Some days I cut out a heart. Other days, I wrote a poem. Occasionally, in the rush of the morning, my notes were mediocre, but I felt strongly that I should always include one. The notes became inside jokes with us — or so I thought.

One day, on the drive home from school, I asked Zoey, "Do you like the notes I write you?"

Perhaps I was having some parental insecurity or it was just a random thought. To my surprise, she replied, "We love them!"

What did she mean by "we?" What she said next inspires me to go the extra mile, even if it seems to be a small matter.

"We all read your notes. We take turns. Sophia, Courtney, Piper, and Emilee. One day the lunch lady who walks around had to tell us a word. She couldn't believe I could read!"

"What do all your friends think of your notes?" I asked, immediately worried they were yanking them from her tiny little hands and mocking her. Perhaps in her naïveté, she wouldn't know if they were making fun of her.

"They L-O-V-E my notes!"

"Oh, good," I said, relieved. I was now very thankful that I had always provided a note, albeit a lame one sometimes.

"Want to know something?" she added.

"What?" I asked, contemplating my new wider audience.

"No matter who reads the note, we always know

how it ends. When we get to the end part, we always say 'Love, Mom' together, really loud!"

"That is a very good thing to remember," I told her.

"We know! It is our favorite part," she replied, tugging her backpack out of the car and smiling at me over her shoulder.

~Amber Chandler

Roots

Be grateful for the home you have, knowing
that at this moment, all you have
is all you need.
~Sarah Ban Breathnach

am the daughter of a master gardener. My mother kneels, dirty, digging, knowing not only where to plant and what, but why. Each spring and summer she nurtures the relationship of soil and seed and sun. Some years I watch, wondering at the work — the weeds and water and endless cultivation of earth. I marvel at the transformation she culls from the depths of half-dead potted plants salvaged from the clearance rack at the nursery. I don't understand this garden, this patient plucking and pruning for fleeting beauty. I don't understand her.

Growing up, I avoided the invitation to sit beside my mother as she planned her plots, as she leafed through catalogs of seeds and stems months before breaking ground. As a late spring frost caressed the stems of the upcoming grass, and I bemoaned the prolonging of winter, my mother prayed the bulbs she planted last year would withstand the weather and the ground would thaw to release life and allow her hands to help it along.

My mother tried to include me despite my disinterest. She bought me an orchid to grow inside. I photographed it and soon forgot it. Each February and March she left the catalogs out where I could browse them, knowing I loved the roses and iris best. When I wanted to arrange flowers she indulged me, allowing me to cut the stems despite my inattention as she tried to explain the flowers and their features. Still, I was indifferent. Gardening was her passion: her dirt, her insects, and her identity… not mine.

As I aged I lost interest in our family's traditional Mother's Day tour of nurseries. I begged my father to let me stay home, to hide in my room with my music. He refused, reminding me of the respect I owed my mother, imploring me not to ruin the moment, the day. I trudged along, unable to understand the allure of the seven varieties of the same plant and how different they could possibly be. Pick one, I thought, and we can go home. What does it matter what you choose?

This year I turned twenty-four, the age my mother was when she married my father. I envision her then as a young woman, free-spirited, with her soft brown eyes concealing a spark. Now I see her in her early eighties, wearing polyester and big-rim glasses that she puts away when she sings, her voice carrying across the living room she shares with my father — a sad but satisfied aria speaking to the dreams she loved but passed up. In the evening she is content to share dinner with a husband who loves her beyond this world, so deeply he'd ask twice for her hand.

And at night, when she lies in bed, her creativity simmers below her sleep, seeking an outlet that will augment the life she's chosen.

This year I go to my parents' lake house, where they are readying the rooms and grounds for rental. I know the final rush is relentless, with days and nights of cleaning, repairing, and prepping. The sky is blue when I arrive despite the sprinkles that followed me for the full forty-five minute drive. My mother is gardening; I grab gloves and stand next to the flowerbed, not knowing plant from weed… not understanding. She says I don't have to, uncertain from years of my avoidance, my apathy. I want to, and I begin to yank the dandelions from the ground, the only weed I recognize as such. She smiles and points out another weed, explaining its invasive roots run as a vine under the surface. As we work, she tells me of dividing plants and the miracle of yielding four or five from one. She shows me how to loosen the root ball at the base of the plant to encourage it to grow; tells me how you have to release the roots to teach them to spread.

As I watch my mother at home in her garden and mimic her movements, I finally understand. I am the daughter of a master gardener. My mother digs deeply through the soil as she cultivates her spirit, her perfectionism put to bed with the bulbs and blossoms, her desire to nurture fulfilled in the foliage of a variegated hosta. She still sings, accompanied by a chorus of clematis and columbine, of black-eyed Susans and Siberian iris and goat's beard. She is a master gardener and her hands have left her heart in the earth and in the roots — and in me.

~Kathryn Roberts

A Promise Is a Promise

A promise is a cloud; fulfillment is rain.
~Arabian Proverb

am a bald woman. It is frightening but also freeing. It is terrifying but also sensual. In reality, it is just very cold. I feel every whisper of wind. I wore hats and bandannas at first — partly to keep warm but mostly to hide my baldness. Secretly I was afraid and wanted to hide.

We discussed her journey — our journey. We listened to all the specialists tell us what was going to happen during her chemotherapy. They talked about all the different kinds of drugs she would take — thirteen in total. They described the ways these drugs would enter her body — some she could take orally, others would have to be injected into her thigh or directly into her spine. Still others would enter the special port that the surgeons had inserted into her chest. The oncologists and nurses talked about the side effects of the drugs and the possible complications that might occur over the next two years of chemotherapy. Two years? She seemed so healthy. How could she be so sick that she needed two years of chemotherapy?

When I told her she had cancer her biggest concern was losing her hair. "Will all my hair really fall out? Will people make fun of me?"

"Don't worry," I told her bravely. "When you lose your hair, I will shave mine and we will both be bald. We will walk down the street proudly with our bald heads held high. We will swim and go to the park and play at the beach with our bald heads."

She pondered this for a minute before responding. "Promise?" she asked with a very serious look on her young little face.

"Promise," I replied matter-of-factly. It seemed

liked such a small sacrifice in comparison to what lay in store for her.

The days and weeks of chemotherapy began to take their toll on her little body. Just as the experts had predicted, she began to lose her hair. It was subtle at first. I began to find strands of hair on her clothes and on towels after she bathed. A short time later, the strands turned into small clumps that I would find on the backs of couches and chairs where she had sat. Before long, there were masses of hair on her pillow every morning as she awoke from her restless sleeps. The time was fast approaching for me to keep my promise. Within a few short days of her pillow being covered in hair each morning she was finally completely bald.

Her head was very smooth and soft as I held her to my breast. Her head felt as smooth as a newborn's skin. It reminded me of that wonderful time when I held her in my arms and marveled at how lucky I was to have such a beautiful and healthy baby girl.

Her bald head was beautiful. Her bald head was

ugly, as the tumors had left their marks. It was time.

She helped shave my head. She held the shaver carefully and moved it over my head row after row. Soon, there was a large pile of golden brown hair glistening in the sunlight on the ground. I, too, was now bald. My head was prickly and harsh. It was ugly. It was beautiful.

All in all, it was a good day; strange but good. It was good to see her smile and run her hands over the top of my head, searching for the hair. It was fun to see her laugh at my baldness. It was strange that this moment of levity was temporary and tempered with the underlying reality that we were both bald because of the terrifying disease of cancer.

We returned home still strangely upbeat from the afternoon's event. As night began to fall, she silently stifled a yawn and asked to go to bed. As I tucked her into bed that night, the good day suddenly took an unexpected turn. As she lay under the covers her normal smiling face turned fearful and she began to cry, clutching her blankets.

"Charlotte, honey, what is the matter?" I asked not understanding what had just happened to cause such fear in her eyes.

"Oh Mommy, you look so scary now with your bald head. I wish you hadn't shaved it," she sobbed.

I didn't know what to say or how to reply. Words failed me and my inner core of strength and courage deserted me in that moment. So I responded the only way I knew how. I cried. I sobbed. I cried for the irony. I cried in self-pity. I cried for the toll it was taking on our family and the impact it was having on our son. I cried and I sobbed.

She didn't say anything but just lay quietly in the soft glow of her bedside lamp and waited patiently for me to stop crying. Then with the wisdom of a five-year-old she reached for my arm and took my hand. She pulled my hand close to her face before resting it upon her cheek.

I felt the warmth of her skin against my wet hands. She sighed and smiled at me. "Don't worry

Mommy," she said softly, "I still love you. Besides, a promise is a promise."

~Tessa Graham

My Mother, My Father, My Everything

All that I am or ever hope to be,
I owe to my angel Mother.
~Abraham Lincoln

t was the happiest day of my life. I was dressed in a long, white gown with a train that filled the room and glass slippers on my feet like Cinderella on her way to the ball. My mother's pearls floated around my neck and an old handkerchief made by my great grandmother resided on my heart. A new veil with scattered pearls to match my dress was tucked into my twists and curls; a borrowed tiara was the perfect accessory and a blue garter was hidden under the layers of fabric, beads and crinoline.

My mother stood where a father should be, beaming with pride. Although I did not have a father to walk me down the aisle, give me away or share the traditional father/daughter dance, I did not feel slighted. My mother had always played both roles as a mother and a father to my brothers and me. She hugged and disciplined us. She helped with homework and shared our joy when we passed a test. She taught us how to love each other even when we were pulling hair or fighting over a toy. She taught us the importance of family. She was, to us, our everything — and still is today.

My husband, Nick, proposed to me when I was twenty-five. My mother asked if I would like my older brother or my uncle to walk me down the aisle. I responded with, "No Mom, you have always been my mom and my dad and you are the only one who can give me away."

The morning of my wedding day passed quickly.

My mother never left my side. She was there for hair, make-up, and helping me put my gown on. Once I was ready, my mom and I stood alone. She was dressed in a long pale blue spaghetti-strapped dress that made her look thirty years younger and more like a bridesmaid than the mother of a twenty-six-year-old bride. She was beautiful. She knew all the right words to say to calm my nerves and assure me that everything would be okay. No one else could have taken her place.

The tears did not begin for either of us until my pastor said it was time for her to give me away. At that moment it became real to both of us; I was really getting married. As we embraced, the room full of people disappeared and it was only my mom and me. Silent promises were exchanged. This is not a farewell, Mom, this is not the end; this is a new beginning and I am not leaving you behind.

Since my mom and I broke all the traditional rules, we kept the theme going with our mother/daughter dance. It was a medley of a few songs that told our story. Starting with "Shall We Dance," a song we often danced to in the kitchen at home, moving onto "Girls Just Want to Have Fun," and finishing with "Last Dance."

My wedding, much like my life, was not ordinary or normal. Thank you, Mom, for teaching me how to laugh when I wanted to cry, encouraging me to write even though I was shy, for loving me with the strength of two parents and above all, for being there.

~Natalie Scott

Standing Out

Courage is being afraid but going on anyhow.
~Dan Rather

I always knew my mom was different from other moms. It wasn't just her appearance — her petite frame, black hair, and dark almond eyes contrasted sharply with the statuesque blondes who accompanied the other kids to school. Her speech was peppered with extra syllables, and sometimes words would come out in the wrong order. It didn't bother me that she was different — after all, I looked different from my friends, too!

On the outside, our house looked like every other house in the neighborhood. But inside, beautiful dolls dressed in colorful kimonos posed in their glass cases. Our refrigerator and cupboards held foods other kids had never seen. I never thought about the significance of these items. They were just a part of my life.

At lunchtime, other kids asked to trade the cookies and candies in their lunches for the rice crackers I brought. And they asked me to show them how to fold squares of paper into little toys like cats, baskets, and birds the way my mom had taught me. If there was any malice directed toward us, my siblings and I were sheltered from it by our wonderful teachers and the other adults in our lives.

The only thing that bothered me was not having relatives nearby. Other kids went to visit their cousins, and talked about their aunts and uncles. My relatives lived on the other side of the world. I knew I had cousins, but I saw them only in pictures. When Mom talked to her sisters on the phone, she used a language that sounded mysterious and fun. At Christmastime, we got beautiful cards embellished with strange looking characters.

It wasn't until I enrolled in a Japanese language class in college that I realized how great an adjustment my mother had made when she followed her husband to his homeland. Until then, Japan was an exotic faraway place, where people spoke differently and ate food that we couldn't find in most Midwest restaurants. Thanks to the international students on campus, I learned more about the customs and culture. In the class I managed to learn several words and phrases, but there were few opportunities to use them once I began my teaching career.

Later on, I became a mom myself. My children inherited my dark hair and eyes, but they were not the only children of Asian descent. By now there were others — children adopted by Caucasian couples, as well as children of immigrants. They, too, were taught to celebrate their differences. When my older daughter was a toddler, my mother and I took her to visit our relatives in Japan. I loved visiting my relatives, but it was frustrating not being able to communicate with them. On shopping trips, my cousins, even though they were younger, watched over me as they would a small child, knowing I couldn't read the street signs or make purchases on my own. Again, I was different. Now I looked like everyone else, but I stood out because I couldn't understand. Was this how Mom felt when she first came to America?

Now that I'm retired from full-time teaching, I have more time to pursue some of my earlier goals. One goal is to learn to speak Japanese fluently. The single year of instruction during my undergraduate years was not enough to carry on a conversation with my aunts and cousins when they came to visit. I want to get to know these relatives. I want to learn about their likes and dislikes, to know about their daily lives, and share stories about our families.

They say it's more difficult to learn a new language after you become an adult, and since I've been an adult for many years, I'd say it's true. But I'm enjoying this new venture. Four days a week,

I sit in a classroom with people less than half my age. Four nights a week, I pore over the exercises and diligently complete the worksheets. It may be more difficult for me to retain the new vocabulary, but I have the time now to do the work and practice. I'm doing this for me, not for a grade. But even more, I'm enjoying the connection to my culture. Every night when I finish my homework, I call my "personal tutor" to check my grammar. She's glad I took on this task. It must have been difficult for her, having to be the interpreter for every visit to Japan, and for each time a relative came to visit. If I become fluent, I can share the burden. But even more, we're building a precious connection to the land she loved and left.

I still think my mom is different. She is different in that she had the courage to leave behind everything she knew and go to a new place and build a new life. She had the intelligence to learn how to assimilate into this unknown society and raise three children, teaching them by example the importance of hard work, perseverance, and respect for others.

I hope I'm different too, and that my kids and grandkids appreciate the difference.

~Patricia Gordon

Whatever You Want To Be

Shoot for the moon. Even if you miss,
you land among the stars.
~Les Brown

My legs swing excitedly, the momentum enough to propel my body off the seat as my pink sneakers scuff the tile floor beneath me. My toothless grin stretches from ear to ear as she places a book that weighs more than I do on the table in front of me. My chubby fingers can't flip the pages quickly enough. My imagination is running wild, creating new tales and carrying me to faraway places faster than I can process.

I am six years old on an early autumn afternoon, sitting at the pattern table at Jo-Ann Fabrics.

Halloween was an event in our house — an event that began well before October thirty-first and far exceeded the simple walk around the neighborhood, sugar highs, and sibling candy bargaining.

Halloween began with a trip to Jo-Ann Fabrics. While many classmates wandered the three aisles at a seasonal costume mecca a week before the holiday, deciding between trendy movie character costumes and clichés in a bag, we'd park ourselves at a local fabric store table and spend hours poring over pattern envelopes and flipping through books.

"Can I be this, Mom?" We'd point to a picture of an outfit far too complex to be replicated by machines and mass-produced for the stores.

"Whatever you want to be," she'd always answer.

While our friends donned witch hats and princess tiaras, we were the Queen of Hearts. Maid Marian. Robin Hood. Snow White. A unicorn. Laura Ingalls

Wilder. A hammerhead shark.

Whatever you want to be.

Our work was done with the selection of a pattern and a request, but for weeks on end, hers continued. After dinner, we'd troop downstairs to play and Mom would retreat to her sewing machine in the corner. We'd hear the buzzing of the sewing machine, punctuated only by the occasional request to try on a sleeve or opine on the angle of a hat.

One day a year, we were allowed to be whatever we wanted to be.

Without even a hint to naïve children, though, her tagline carried over into everyday life. When I wanted to be an actress, I was one. As I pranced onstage, Dad built the production's sets and Mom sewed costumes. Eleven sequined showgirl costumes by Thursday? Whatever you (and your friends) want to be. When my sister wanted to be a Division One college athlete, we piled into the car for practices across the state and tournaments across several. When my brother wanted to be a high-jump star, they huddled under blankets for hours for a two-second spurt of activity.

Eventually, we moved out of the house and began our own lives. College majors changed daily, and the refrain was always the same.

Mom, I want to major in English.

You've always had impeccable grammar. Whatever you want to be, you'll do well.

Maybe special education is the right choice.

You've always been so good with kids — your patience will serve you well in that profession. Whatever you want to be, your dad and I will support you.

I'm going to be a writer.

We've always said that's your gift. Whatever you want to be, we'll always buy your books.

I'm sure Mom groaned to herself each time we veered off track, gravitating toward the intricate (and occasionally downright bizarre) costume patterns and low-paying (and occasionally dead-end) careers. But she gritted her teeth just the same, and worked her magic.

Hindsight is always 20/20. As I look back on my childhood today, I recognize that mantra as the cornerstone of a remarkable woman. A woman who, despite the ever-blowing winds of change that accompany the rearing of three children, knew that her one task was to love us, unconditionally. Love us — and occasionally, tolerate us — and support us, whatever path or persona we chose. Whether we wanted to be a pink satin unicorn or a black velvet hammerhead shark.

~Caitlin Q. Bailey O'Neill

Mother or Daughter?

The doors we open and close each
day decide the lives we live.
~Flora Whittemore

The hospital woke me before sunrise and told me that my mother was dying. It was the day my daughter was leaving our home in New York to spend a year in Israel. We had lost her father only months earlier so my being with her was doubly important. My mom was deathly ill in an ICU in St. Louis. I didn't know where to be, who to sacrifice. Was I mother or daughter? I didn't think I could be both.

If we didn't pack, Natasha wasn't going. That much was simple. But while every other kid in the program was awakened with kisses and farewell waffles in bed, or so I imagined, my daughter got, "Get up. We need to pack right now because I may be leaving for St. Louis." It wasn't fair, but as any eleventh grader who's lost her daddy will tell you... life isn't.

It has been a fact of my daughter's life that I have parents who are ill and live a thousand miles away. There are phone calls in the night, missed choir performances, last minute changes to plans, and a mom whose brain is not always fully engaged in what happened today in math class. I love her more than words can express, but sometimes I just have to go. This has always been hard, but even more so in the past year, while we are still reeling from the loss of my husband, her father.

While packing her bags — nine T-shirts, one pair of rain boots, a jar of peanut butter — I took calls from the hospital and tried to decide where I belonged. I agreed to have my mother put on a respirator — two hooded sweatshirts, two sets of sheets, three bottles of sunblock — and weighed the duffle bags to be sure that each one was exactly fifty pounds.

I tried to make Natasha's last day at home as pleasant as possible — blood pressure 50/30, kidneys failing, heart rate plummeting — and worked in a break for iced coffee and brownies. Periodically I went into the bathroom and cried.

By the time my daughter's bags were packed, I realized I had made a decision. It broke a part of my heart but it was crystal clear. I couldn't send my daughter alone to an airport departure lounge filled with mothers and fathers, sisters and brothers, balloons and goodbye banners. I needed to help check her luggage, buy her a magazine, give her a hug — or many hugs — and send her off. I prayed that my mother would be there when I got to St. Louis but acknowledged that she would probably not be. I hoped that whatever happened, I would be able to forgive myself. And I said goodbye to my mother.

I took my daughter to the airport and said goodbye to her too. A different goodbye — a less permanent goodbye — but in its way, just as jarring. As soon as she was out of sight I flew to St. Louis. And miraculously, my mother made it. She might so easily not have. It takes matters too far to say that if she hadn't, I would have believed unswervingly that I made the right decision. But in that horrible case, I hope that with time I would have come to realize that, in deciding to be a mother first, I was being true to my mom too.

A friend told me once that by caring for my parents I was role-modeling behavior that my daughter should learn. "You're teaching her to take care of your old bones someday," is how she put it. I hope not.

We raise our sons and our daughters, not for our own succor, but to see them grow into loves and lives of their own. And hopefully, having children of their own whom we watch them raise and nurture all over again. And while no person should ever face what my mother did alone, perhaps she took comfort from the fact that I honored everything she has been to me and everything she has taught me, by caring for my daughter first. I learned from her what a mother should be.

~Jacqueline Rivkin

A Mother's
Last Lecture

*The best way to stop smoking is to just
stop — no ifs, ands or butts.*
~Edith Zittler

It was the day after winter break when Belinda walked up to my desk, silently handing me a note. It was from her mother, requesting a parent-teacher conference. I quickly wrote her back, setting up a time for the following afternoon right after dismissal.

I was actually anxious to meet her, as she had been unable to attend the initial back-to-school night. Belinda was an excellent student, although the past five weeks her grades had dropped dramatically. The scheduled conference would give us a chance to discuss the situation.

At 3:45, Belinda's mother, Mrs. K., arrived. She was an attractive, although rail-thin, woman who proffered a sad, almost melancholy smile before sitting. When she spoke, her voice was soft, almost hoarse. "Nice to meet you," she said.

"And you as well. I enjoy getting to know my students' parents."

She folded her hands in her lap, a tissue twisted in between them. "I guess you know Belinda's grades have been dropping."

I nodded. "She does seem a bit preoccupied."

"Yes, and I wanted to talk to you about that." She leaned forward a moment, suddenly overcome with a harsh cough. "Sorry," she said, pointing to her throat. "This is the reason for Belinda's change."

Puzzled, I stared back at her, unable to decipher her meaning.

"You see, Belinda's worried about my health. In

late November I learned that I have lung cancer."

I sat back in my chair, stunned by her news.

Seeing the obvious shock on my face, Mrs. K. reached out and touched my hand. "The prognosis is poor. But these past few weeks I've truly come to grips with it and I hope — I pray — that Belinda has too.

"For years my family warned me about my smoking, but I just laughed it off. I mean, my God, I'm only forty-one years old! Even the constant coughing couldn't convince me to stop. So when the doctor told me I had lung cancer, this did not come as a total shock to them."

"My sole regret is that I won't see my baby grow up. Belinda's been so supportive of me. Now, I want to do something for her — and her classmates. Mr. Chaney, I want to explain the evils of smoking and I want to include your class."

I sat there a moment, dumbfounded, unable at first to comprehend the courageous deed she had offered to me. This was something that could conceivably be much more effective than having the class read statistical data on smoking from a textbook. I asked her what she had in mind.

"Well, I'd like to talk to your fifth period health class since Belinda is in it. I thought I could come in from time to time and talk to them about my progression. And I'd like to do this for as long as I can. What do you think?"

"I'll need the okay from my principal, but that shouldn't be a problem."

She nodded, stood, shook my hand again and turned to go. "Look forward to seeing you soon."

Having gotten permission, Mrs. K. arrived the following Friday, neatly dressed but looking even thinner than she had at our earlier meeting. I looked at Belinda, sitting in the second row, noting both pride, and weariness etched on her face. I introduced her and explained the reason for her visit. The class gave perfunctory applause as she approached the front of the class. She began her lecture by saying, "Hi, I'm Beth, Belinda's mom and I have lung cancer."

You could have heard the proverbial pin drop. Kids who usually were half-tuned in to what I was saying suddenly sat upright. Mrs. K. paused a moment, stifled yet another cough and proceeded to tell the class about her twenty-six-year history of smoking.

She discussed peer pressure and the need to "look cool." It didn't take long, she said before that stage gave way to lighting up whenever she felt stressed or needed a quick pick-me-up. Finally, all that became immaterial when she realized, all too late, that she was hooked and needed her nicotine fix. Afterwards, she took questions; then she indicated she would be back the following week.

As she left I wondered just how many of my eighth grade students were totally convinced by her straightforward talk.

The following session she brought with her a set of X-rays. Drawing the students out of their seats they approached tentatively, staring at the dark spots that Mrs. K. stated were cancer. This seemed to hit home even harder than her earlier talk. She stayed only a few minutes, as she was not feeling well, but she promised to return the following week. Looking around I noticed the students all appeared quite somber and remained that way throughout the rest of the period.

For the next three weeks, Mrs. K. was forced to cancel her talks, due to ill health and doctors' appointments. However, the next week, she reappeared. She seemed more gaunt than ever, her dress hanging on her, huge circles under her eyes. She spent forty minutes discussing her feelings about family support. This time no one questioned her. It appeared my students were becoming as drained as she, obviously affected by her lectures. Belinda, however, was not. Resolve had replaced her earlier misery and with each passing day, I couldn't help but admire her courageous demeanor.

In April, Mrs. K. brought in another set of X-rays showing how the cancer was quickly spreading. She could no longer stand so she addressed the class from a chair. Her coughing remained consistent throughout the lecture but she discussed how she kept up her daily routine, which, much to our chagrin, meant smoking throughout the day whenever possible.

She came again in May, speaking only in a whisper, and pulling a canister of oxygen behind her. Mrs. K. talked about how she and her doctor had discussed hospice care and pain control. She ended by saying she hoped to be back soon but as soon as she got up, the students rose from their chairs, surrounded her and hugged her. Then she left.

During the end of May, she called to say she'd like to come in one more time, as she wanted to end her lectures by asking the kids how many intended to smoke after what they'd heard and seen. But on the day she was to come in I noticed Belinda was not in class. During my lunch hour I called the house and the husband answered. He informed me that his wife had passed away the night before. Shaken, I offered my condolences.

The next day, as my fifth period health class entered, I informed them of the news. I also told them that Mrs. K.'s last request was to ask how many of the students still intended to smoke. "Class," I said, "after what you've witnessed these past few months with Belinda's mom, how many of you still intend to smoke, either now or in the future? Raise your hand if you do."

Not a soul moved. Belinda's mother had done her job well.

~J.D. Chaney

The Rest Is Unwritten

*Turn your face to the sun and the
shadows fall behind you.*
~Maori Proverb

can't believe I am doing this again. I am crying hysterically, hidden behind the closed bathroom door at work.

I seem to have it together everywhere else, but every time I come into work a dark, hellacious shadow invades my view. I don't belong here, yet I can't seem to find a way out. I have to face it — I hate my job!

I am in a role that does not play to any of my strengths. Every day I keep hoping my boss will recognize my good ideas and promote me, but I feel invisible here. Less than a year ago, I was making four times as much money, I was in a leadership role, and I was doing work that I loved. Then I was laid off. Now I am stuck in a dead-end job that I can't find any passion for. I look into the bathroom mirror and splash water on my face. I say to myself, "Get it together girl, you are living through the largest economic depression since the 1930s; be happy you even have a job."

I pull myself together long enough to finish my shift. As I exit my workplace, I gaze across the shopping center and see a beautiful version of what I'll likely look like in thirty years. To my amazement, my mother is approaching me. Before I can even ask what she's doing here, she explains: "I had a feeling you needed a friend today. So I cleared my schedule and came to say hi! Are you off work now?" I reach out for one of her world famous hugs, and say, "Mom, you are so amazing; your timing couldn't be better. Lets go get dinner."

For the past few months, my job situation has gone from okay to horrible. My mother has patiently listened as I've shared how things keep getting worse. As we sit down for dinner I go over the details of my day, but exclude the tale of my bathroom breakdown. Before I can finish the story, my mother reaches across the booth, grabs my hands and says, "What would it take… how much money would you need, to get peace of mind and quit? I'm convinced that you are blocking your true self by staying in this toxic environment."

As the words come out of her mouth, a weight miraculously lifts off my shoulders. I answer, "I have enough money in savings to hold me over until I find a job!" At this moment, I realize I have been trapping myself. No one is keeping me in this painful job except for me. My mother just reminded me that in life we always have choices. I can choose to be happy. One small comment from my mother opened the space in my mind to have a transformational shift. I realize that up until now, I have been making excuses, finding reasons to justify dealing with my unhappiness instead of seeking to change my circumstances. I just couldn't see the way out through the fear that was consuming me. My mother helped peel the blinders back.

I take my mother's advice and put in my two-week notice at work. My manager tells me that when I walked into work that day, I exuded a calm presence that she hadn't seen in me before. I don't want to tell her that the reason for my changed mood was that I finally felt free and alive again. When I tell her "I quit!" I don't just mean quitting this job. Internally, I understand that I'm also quitting my routine of excuses and justification. From now on, I resolve that I will always choose love over fear. Of course, I don't say any of this to my manager. Instead I simply smile and say, "Thank you for this opportunity, but I've realized that it is my time to leave."

As I push through the last two weeks in this job, I try to leave the fear behind. I try to trust in my safety net, but the reality is that I do not have another job lined up and I begin to worry. I feel that I'm taking a giant leap of faith. What if I don't get a job for months? The anxiety creeps back in. Precisely at that moment I get a text message from my mom. It reads, "Trust your heart; you are doing the right thing. Today is the first day of the rest of your life; the rest is still unwritten." I smile at my mother's words, and realize she is right; everything is in divine order. It seems like my mother's timing is yet again perfect. Literally five minutes after my mother's message I receive a phone call from my future employers. They want me to start full-time as soon as possible… making twice my current income!

I am immediately filled with gratitude. My mother was the guiding light who helped me get back on track. Mothers have a way of knowing and guiding when we go astray. I needed a wake-up call. My mother swooped in at the moment I most needed her to shower me with her wisdom and love.

~Shannon Kaiser

Meet Our Contributors

Amber Chandler is a middle school English teacher in Hamburg, NY. She is inspired by her children Zoey and Oliver, but especially by her husband Matt. She'd like to thank her mother-in-law Chris, who is the stay-at-home Nana, allowing Amber to pursue her dreams.

J.D. Chaney is a retired teacher, published novelist and freelance writer. He lives in the Bay Area with his wife and 17-year-old daughter. His hobbies include traveling, running, reading and watching his beloved San Francisco Giants.

Jan Cline is a freelance writer, speaker and writers'

conference director from Spokane Valley, WA. She leads a writing group in her area and enjoys golf, traveling and grandchildren. Jan has had many articles and short stories published. Learn more about her at www.jancline.net.

Patricia Gordon is a retired elementary school teacher, mother and grandmother. She holds teaching degrees from Illinois State University and Western Michigan University. She now teaches music education at Grand Valley State University and loves to write about her family. She also writes fiction as Patricia Kiyono.

Tessa Graham works for the BC provincial government and writes in her spare time. She has been published in *Island Parent*, *Today's Parent* and *Pacific Yachting*. Shortly after her daughter's diagnosis, she and her husband began to plan for the family's future. In 2009/10, they took a sabbatical and moved to southwest France (http://talesfromouryearinfrance. blogspot.com).

Shannon Kaiser is an inspirational travel writer, author, adventure junkie and art director. Shannon is founder of playwiththeworld.com, an adventure site dedicated to helping others love life fully. Connect with her there.

Mimi Greenwood Knight is a mama of four living in South Louisiana with her husband David and way too many pets. She's blessed to have over 500 essays and articles in magazines, anthologies and on websites including in over twenty *Chicken Soup for the Soul* books. She enjoys gardening, baking, birding and Bible study.

Mary Elizabeth Laufer has a degree in English Education from SUNY Albany. As a Navy wife and mother of two, she moved around the country for twenty years, working in schools and libraries. Her stories have been published in magazines, newspapers and anthologies. She lives in St. Cloud, FL.

Caitlin Q. Bailey O'Neill has previously been published in two other *Chicken Soup for the Soul* books. When not reminiscing on a fairytale childhood, she enjoys photography, theater, gardening, and spending time with her husband Chris and her family. Caitlin can be reached via e-mail at PerfectlyPunctuated@yahoo.com.

Jacqueline Rivkin lives in New York City with her teenage daughter, Natasha, also a writer. Jacqueline has a master's degree from the Columbia University Graduate School of Journalism and has contributed to publications including *Newsday, Self* and *Jet*. This is her third essay in the *Chicken Soup for the Soul* series.

Kathryn Roberts lives and writes in Portland, ME. She received her BFA degree in Creative Writing and English Literature from Goddard College. Her work has appeared in various publications including *NAP Literary Magazine*, *Girls' Life* magazine, and the *Sun Journal*.

Natalie Scott received her Bachelor of Arts degree in English with a concentration in Journalism from the University of Delaware in 2005. She is a writer for Easter Seals. She is married to Nicholas Scott and they have a daughter named Eleanora Lynn who has preceded her to heaven.

Meet Amy Newmark

Amy Newmark is the best-selling author, editor-in-chief, and publisher of the *Chicken Soup for the Soul* book series. Since 2008, she has published 140 new books, most of them national bestsellers in the U.S. and Canada, more than doubling the number of Chicken Soup for the Soul titles in print today. She is also the author of *Simply Happy*, a crash course in Chicken Soup for the Soul advice and wisdom that is filled with easy-to-implement, practical tips for having a better life.

Amy is credited with revitalizing the Chicken

Soup for the Soul brand, which has been a publishing industry phenomenon since the first book came out in 1993. By compiling inspirational and aspirational true stories curated from ordinary people who have had extraordinary experiences, Amy has kept the twenty-four-year-old Chicken Soup for the Soul brand fresh and relevant.

Amy graduated *magna cum laude* from Harvard University where she majored in Portuguese and minored in French. She then embarked on a three-decade career as a Wall Street analyst, a hedge fund manager, and a corporate executive in the technology field. She is a Chartered Financial Analyst.

Her return to literary pursuits was inevitable, as her honors thesis in college involved traveling throughout Brazil's impoverished northeast region, collecting stories from regular people. She is delighted to have come full circle in her writing career — from collecting stories "from the people" in Brazil as a twenty-year-old to, three decades later, collecting stories "from the people" for Chicken Soup for the Soul.

When Amy and her husband Bill, the CEO of Chicken Soup for the Soul, are not working, they are visiting their four grown children.

Follow Amy on Twitter @amynewmark. Listen to her free daily podcast, The Chicken Soup for the Soul Podcast, at www.chickensoup.podbean.com, or find it on iTunes, the Podcasts app on iPhone, or on your favorite podcast app on other devices.

Changing lives one story at a time ®
www.chickensoup.com